Y, ES&
DIAERESIS

Also by Demosthenes Agrafiotis

Poetry Networks 3, Translations from the Greek of Demosthenes Agrafiotis and Nikos Phokas, Poetry at Annagh makerrig, (Translators: K. Newmann, P. Boran, T. Curtis, Th. Dorgan), Dedalus Press, Dublin, 1994.

Poetry-Paparty, New Yipes Reader No 23, Oakland, Editor, David Larsen, 10/2007, 50 pages (texts, images, photographies, drawings). California, 2008.

Monogatari II, English – Japanese poems and drawings of Harumi Tecao, Taiyo-Koshiky, pocket edition, Nagoya, 2008.

Maribor (Tr. Angelos Sakkis and John Sakkis), The Post Apollo Press, California, U.S.A., 2010, 15X21 cm 88 pages (poemus and two fotos).

Chinese Notebook, (Tr. Angelos Sakkis and John Sakkis), Ugly Duckling Press, N.Y., U.S.A. 2010, bilingual.

Artxart, Redfoxpress, Achill Island, Ireland, 2011. Franticham's Assembling Box Nr. 8, Visual Poetry and works influenced by Fluxus, Redfoxpress, Ireland, 2010.
± graphies," Veer Books, London, no 36, 2011.

ArtxArt, Images – Collages, texts – fotos, section: "c' est mon dada," Redfoxpress, Ireland.

A/Ω. Beans Abecedary, Franticham's Assembling Box, no 15, Visual Poetry and Works inspired by Fluxus, 23 artists, 10/2011, Redfoxpress, Ireland.

"now, 1/3" & thepoem (Tr. John Sakkis and Angelos Sakkis), BlazeVOX, Buffalo, NY.

bebeDADA, Artist' s book, Estepa Editions, Paris, 2015.

Y,es, in Japanese and in English, Artist 's book, (translation: Hejime Ishida and John Sakkis/Angelos Sakkis), drawings (ink) Tkesada Matsutani,Estepa Editions, Paris, 2015.

Y, ES&
DIAERÉSIS

DEMOSTHENES AGRAFIOTIS

Some poems in this collection have appeared in
Seedlings, 2016 edited by Jerrold Shiroma.

Layout and Book Design: DUSIE
dusie.org | Kingston, RI

Cover image: Demosthenes Agrafiotis

First printing, 2016.

Translated from the Greek: Angelos Sakkis and
John Sakkis

ISBN: 978-1-944253-01-1

LIBRARY OF CONGRESS NUMBER: 2015960903

Y, ES & DIAERESIS

DEMOSTHENES AGRAFIOTIS

TRANSLATION FROM THE GREEK:
ANGELOS SAKKIS AND JOHN SAKKIS

CONTENTS

Y,

n
ni
nig
nigh
night
nights without the help
        of temporary personnel.

plus
solution
without?

geographic distances
the luxury of weighing
                toward and by

minus
fact
the

notice the lost examples

pure antagonism.

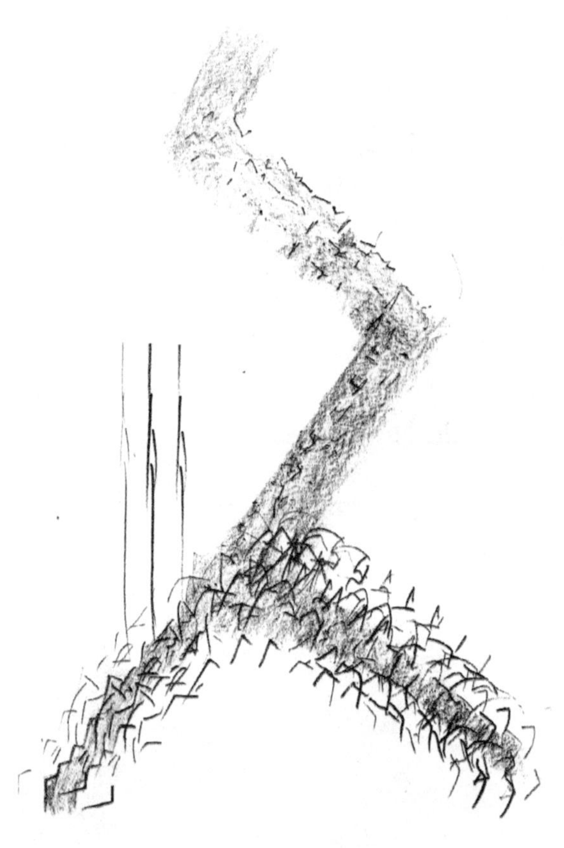

eenie, meenie
zippy-dippy
(other idioms)

thus and otherwise

speakable, yet uncertain
what
why not

signature.

of artificial deviations
such as
however
and what's quiet
and what words do

Le Bar

and what letters do.

hokum
pokum
sokum

and other companies

notices from the cashier's office

voids
of naked bodies – and the clouds

paratactic lethargy.

u   topia
dis
para
dia
hetero   topia

Ici demeura
De 1822 a 1827
Jean Capodistrias De Corfu
Ministre de Czar Alexandre I
aux Congres de Vienne et de Paris
Gouverneur elu de la Grece affranchie
Citoyen de Geneve et de Lausanne

      dissonance

exercises of flexible space vectors

      luxury of the diaspora.

*t*ime

> *i*nflow regardless of the

drea*m* of another language
> signals

pand*e*monium.

mouths
psi-ψ?
plastic flowers

travelers on over-
                passes.

child
Oh!
delirium.

lightly, lightly

days of strolling

taming of these ones

but gently.

I flicker

plus
plus, minus
minus

slander from the living
     about the age of the planets.

econ.
sch.
mass med.

night-time conspiracy
arrangement of the re-broadcasts
and the rest

unarchic

inadequate glory of abbreviations.

O, o

waters
prizes of the hunt

(the afternoon)

en plein ciel.

the spaces of craftsmen

Genzi, Kenzi

thinned-out branches of weeping willow
river

stories of *Gion*

remembrance; adolescent (vague)
charges

pyrotechnics

the children can't ma-
    nage the pyres
        and the nasal sounds.

obligations
readjustments

waves, waves

the territory is offered
from, with, by, for

ambiguities.

weighing of ink
ow
ouch

round impressions
of one
and

along with.

palindromes *revisited*

reversal, care

chain-linked chairs
block the aggressive stares

"La revue musicale"

--dedication, for the anemics
of peripheral aristocracy
to be kept alive

luckily those who teach
leave the horizon of memory

separations, origin
the first impression
     history of passions.

Ah!
only ah

definitely.

the   end   x
all the curlicues

tombs of nations.

contrariness

Horace, Horace

the search for the atypical
    and the dyst(r)opic.

givemethekey
white   p
           l
           a
           z
           a

the glance
abhors   the
                or
ders.

of coffee
and the anorexic nature

eviction
unification

collection
oblique glances.

the secret?

Formulla in Restauro
Panel under Restauration
Orfeo (La poesia)

the bridges teach indifference

bicycles in disrepair

rivers flow into the minimum
divisors of the day

the hope.

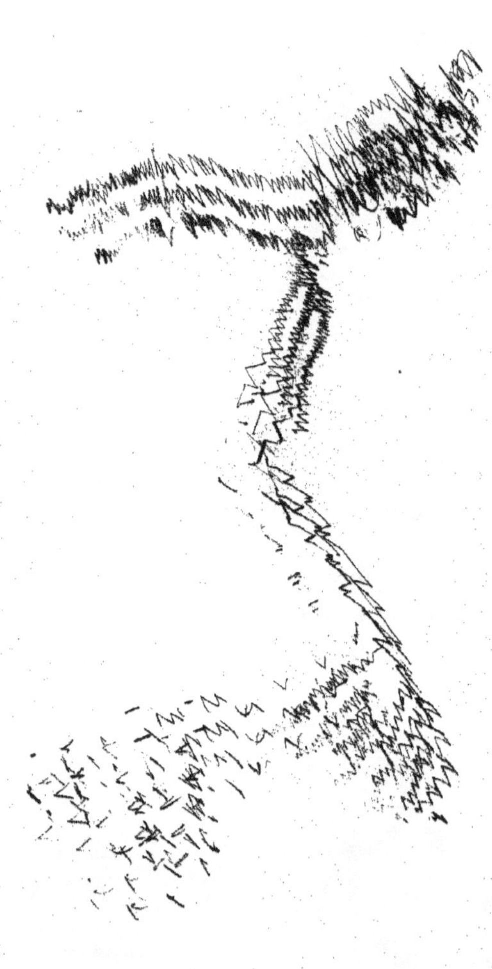

unholy

                       engagement
                   in enchanted
                     encounter

surface, dissent

language remittances

(counterfeit)
for the deductions of
      reciprocity.

Borgo De Greci

Βαβαί τίνος γαρ εικών
(Alack but whose likeness)

       worth it though
sparkle

Autoritratto —
Antonio Moro (1517 – 1576)

the admiration, to be sure

otherwise what would be the voyage
      and what the exceptions?

the time
of time
in time
oh time

30" for the writing
10" for the reading.

brilliancy
in apprenticeship
    without proper
    observations

comma

,

hunched
constellations
    of muscovite isinglass
    and now.

applause
self-evident

inspiration
and
those.

it belongs
without starting

continuation

experiential word hunt

the hope that winter will hold
leads to the style

how
where; where?
how?

      the action
      an assessment
      of fate, namely barriers.

sound-producing
sound-consuming
sound-analytical
    essay

space not only
    recognizable

condensation
    co-ordinates.

conviction
distortions

Non
holy
          bizarre
                    assessment.

the decency of the early news

distillation of red
without motions of the body

coffee shops in a parallel universe:
                    carte blanche.

letters are lost with
a gesture and repris-
als are exacted be-
fore the last bus

the memory of the
country opens to the
day with the glance on
catalogues and regist. #

with a gesture are lost.

in basements of glory

just as

not

the latest edition

again

no

the final version.

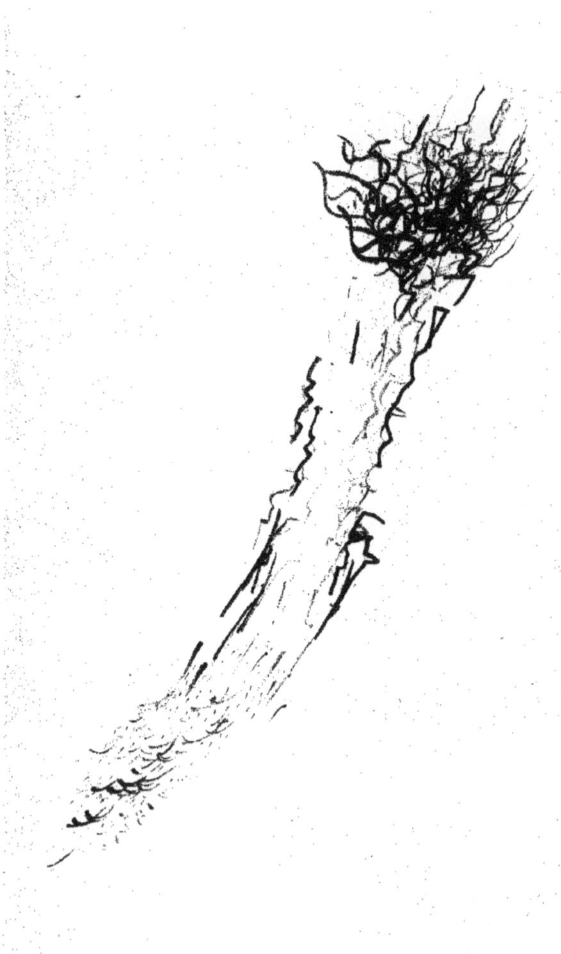

Corpo Incorrotto
Di S. Antonino Prelozzi
1389 –1459 Fondatore del Convento
Di S. Marco. Riformatore
Del Ordine Domenicano
Arcivescovo et Patrone di Firenze

worms and unidirectional procedures
so that the orders are kept unfulfilled

Ecce Filias Tuns (sic)

ultimate lesson before the error.

in those very words
(or close to)

leaps of joy at morning openings
placing of the dreams inside con-
ventional window displays talons
of predatory disappointment

cities where the implements
                    can hide.

it starts with a capital letter

the appearances of the crowd
in elastic screens

long-term arrangement
        according to values.

there

the weight
the forecast

without springs

"drop coin or words here"

entropy.

for Tom Raworth

x2-a2 = (x+a)(x-a)

identity.

keys, rhapsodies

genitomania

may aphrodisiac matters be reconciled
            with the chlamys
            and lakefront cities.

"rejoice and rejoice"

he got up
he
stop
ped
at the great road

aspects not commented upon.

loose parallels

to calibrate the tongues
            the languages
in combination with the traces
of one the same
and the same
            alike.

don't, no
yes, no

for certain

this way
and that

consequences.

In Queste Stanza
Vissa E Mori
Maria Maddalena De Pazzi
Amante Dell' Amore Di Cristo

and all the oscillations as
they run to Venice for mistresses or lovers

calculating the lost glances
(once in a while) the failures are disregarded

                              preferences
concessions

the bicycle laps interrupt
the continuity of memories.

letters no longer arrive
            from Attica

stagnation
nightly (aphasia)

privative   *ω.*

poor presence
a sideways π
reference to other
            names.

thirst

through, throughout the media

(as in "throughout a vacation")

           conceptions
           open seas

stevedores of yesterday's message.

"listen to how he talks"

irregularities in the garden
    with venerable letters

expression, excoriation.

writing; like

wagons lits

the street of the old city
opens with austere invocations

c, ∂, G, e, ∂, L

the burden of generations
with necessary struggles

"La clémence"

afternoon and lethargy

departure.

coexistence of the proverb with weariness

slow learning of the motions

body

parallel circulations
in spaces of the fragile geology

disgraceful digitals

announcements block the accumulation.

the waiting
is dedicated
to the theo(re)ms or sup(re)macy

u
  p
  r
o
a
  r

vital education
for so many exchanges.

and other without
what more
for

the pleasure

49

company
Swiss interest rates.

drenched evening
may the only (even if feeble) answer be given
to the calling of favorable rhythms

the moments forebode the reversals
of the species

carnal pleasure

elegy?

Ristorante Campidoglio.

            s
        o
        r
      t*i*me
      a
    k
slippages
uneasy days
            in winter

or

        ros
        t*i*me
    ka
slippages
uneasy days
        of winter.

not   all

all with no

e

froth of the decorations.

and may the difference be
and may not the difference be
                    and not

and the partitions are not sufficient

construction of wholes with uncertain
                    congruencies

                    and as

the dilemmas are judged.

la maison

the conductibles

call for
concern
concentration
contempt

comestibles

colonial goods.

trenches
    factions
    waves

"verb, verb"

they cannot even be granted.

intra-seasonal leaps of joy
bare beginnings (to the nth degree)
comparisons of parts

the two possibilities

sterilizations or transfers
of the consonants

vowe-liminations

passions
in bulletins

are released.

es

DIAERESIS

(pre-historic sorrow)

curled up in a diaphanous
                    shell
I am indifferent
to knowledge
to usage
I stir only
for distances
     the emptying of images
          into the great maw.

searching

> drawers of toys
> attics of images

apportionment of the bodies in new
> foundations

> unity
> grammar

acceptance of the fragmentation.

samples
gaps in catalogs
typeset curses

a fact
separated from its value.

strolls in the neighborhoods
the touch destroys the continuities

gaps in the body
nuances of color rot away because of inertia

exaggeration of yearnings.

I was gaaaazing
at the closing of the broken lines

but the horse races require
distances and results.

confirmation   execution

on the wager of the shared points
the lists of workers are ignored

(utopia)

surfaces
prohibiting signs
books full of holes

everything is burning

deluge   of repetitions.

you need me for the deviation
you call me and you don't call me
you beckon
and then you push me away

worthless both of us.

(scheduled carnal pleasures)

I too a stool pigeon of discontinuity
I don't pronounce all the words.

pinball machines are tamed
with pictures or slug coins

mastery with fingers and words

so long as there is no blackout
or the coffee shop isn't filled with leaves.

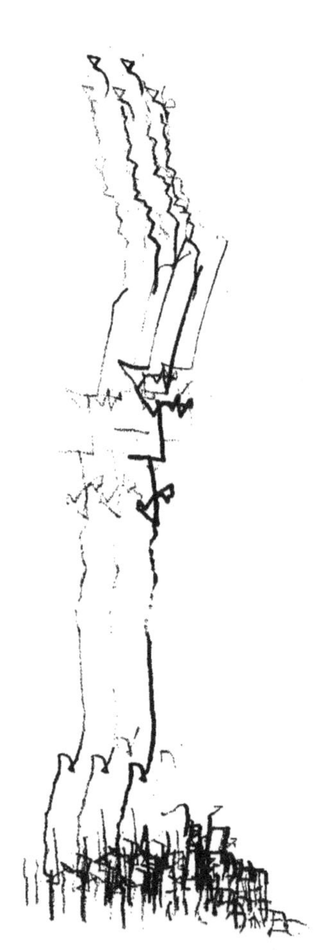

glances pass you by
they are directed

to what   is magnified and
                      multiplied.

you mediate
the forgery of glances
the indifference in front of the mirror

but still you search for arguments
when fear paralyzes your throat
you miserable radio announcer.

saw dust from faces

the coffee shops are filled with crystals
writing is not enough

I lurk on overpasses

exposing
my shriveled limbs

auctioning off
my affectations

so I won't bite my fellow citizens.

the hoarders of what's left behind
unbutton their vests

the alchemists hide backstage.

magnitude   sarcasm
the directions   are trapped

desire   manner
memories are sold off in the balconies.

the settlers
on the island of cedars and skeletons
lower the window blinds

Marika's red cheeks.

protection, prediction
persistence in front of the mirror

(the immigrant dared go out to the window
display)

and above all
attentiveness to stone constructions.

(capitulation through glances)

proof

that in the territory of fear
   neither jabs nor ebullience will do.

window display full of

>   blue gas
>   collection of glass eyes
>   shadows

the pilgrims   admire

>   for a few clothes-pins
>   they offer whatever is left
>   of their kindness.

(conspiracy)

When graph tables and charts crush you
you scream
that everything is the same
and then you draw the line of addition.

the selling-off of garbage
deluge of insinuations
hatching of sounds

tomorrow the parade.

trees   color hues
offshoots block the   passageways

precious metals   borders
the inspectors at customs keep an eye
                    on the percentages

guards and gales   on alert.

a little soil

for the menders of molecules
        the boiler-men of averages
for the naked.

tedious is the word of death

and its disposal suffocating
when the thief of final assessments
hides his name in every meeting
                in every line of words.

the activities are served with newspapers

tactics   planning

bon appetit

special missions   shortage of blood.

noises
successive reclining
stained bed sheets

the rooms absorb the differences

the actions

smoothing of surfaces
distortion of mass

kairos – a time comes

the sound
shatters the dream

falling back without successions.

chewing gum

the words

    fuel of repetition
    carnivorous birds of materiality
    blades for chopping tobacco.

moments of cheapness

next time
imitate a single pang of conscience.

the saliva makes flags
and the tongue pushes
the sprouted words   special orders

                of dwarfs
                of word endings
                of those of the same religion
                of the self-
                determined

the error though is not with writing.

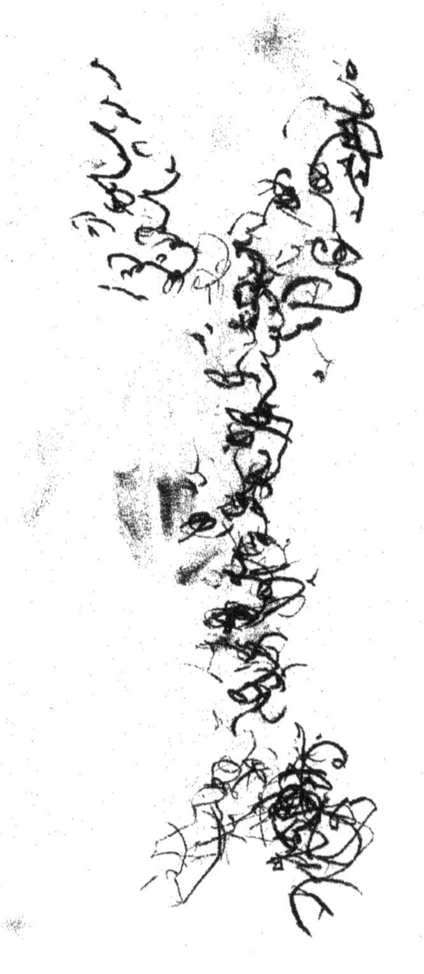

attention to signs
stations are not taken into account

(merchandise
insurance policies, exchanges)

now
weeping behind the stairs
the purchase of disintegration with private
projections

enlargements   imprints   and   words
recognition   result

you   orientate   knots   and   lines
fatigue   and   indifference.

since the words are emptied out

may the minor tremors
be saved
and the remainders of *triaeresis*.

(polypheria)

around the wrestling mat
wrinkles
suicides
piles of lemon wedges

the glance   creates   rules
when the airborne field of axioms
                    is seeded with eyes.

stars   lights
paper   ornaments   ambitions

dropped underwear   parentheses.

loudspeakers
dilapidated telephones

let's play our cowardice
on a dreidel.

much better

the dissolution
the breathing rhythms after
     the gesture of rejection
the enunciation of the first and
     last word.

DEMOSTHENES AGRAFIOTIS is active in the fields of poetry/ painting/photography/ intermedia/ installation and the way they interact. He has a special interest in the relation between art and new technologies. His book *Maribor* (The Post-Apollo Press) was awarded the 2011 Northern California Book Award for Poetry in Translation, *Chinese Notebook* (Ugly Duckling Presse) appeared later that same year, *"now, 1/3" & thepoem* (BlazeVOX Books) was published in 2012, all three books were translated by Angelos and John Sakkis. His recent books are +graphies (Veer Books), Betises (Editions Fidel Anthelme X), and ArtxArt (Redfoxpress). He is based in Athens, Greece.

ANGELOS SAKKIS was born in Greece. He immigrated to California in 1970 and received his BFA at San Francisco Art Institute in 1989. He translates Greek poetry to English and has co-translated the work of poet and multimedia artist Demosthenes Agrafiotis with John Sakkis numerous times. His own work has appeared in *Ambush Review, Try* and *Hellenic Voices*. His chapbooks *Memory-of* and *Fictional Character* were published by Zarax Books, 2012. *Travel log with Homer on my mind 2011* was published by BOTH BOTH, 2012. With Jack Hirschman he translated *Food Line* by Sotirios Pastakas, Forepaw Press, 2015. Most recently he participated in Cross Section, an Anthology of Contemporary Greek Poetry, Erato Press. He lives in Oakland, California.

JOHN SAKKIS is the author of *RAVE ON!*, recently released by BOTH BOTH; *The Islands* published by Nightboat Books in 2015 and *Rude Girl*, BlazeVOX Books, 2009. With Angelos Sakkis he has translated many books by Athenian poet Demosthenes Agrafiotis: their translation of Agrafiotis's *Maribor*, The Post-Apollo Press, 2011, was awarded the 2011 Northern California Book Award for Poetry in Translation.He Lives in Oakland.

SIE
DU